3 4882 10108 7220

D1368736

ONE INCREDIBLE DOG!

BOONE

WRITTEN BY CHRIS WILLIAMS
ILLUSTRATED BY JUDITH FRIEDMAN

Published by Moo Press, Inc.
Warwick, New York

The text of this book is set in 14 point Adobe Bookman, with drop caps in Goudy Stout. Cover and book design by Judith Friedman. The illustrations are done in graphite with watercolor accents.

BVG 10 9 8 7 6 5 4 3 2 1

Library Cataloging-in-Publication Data

Williams, Chris.
One Incredible Dog! Boone/Chris Williams;
illustrated by Judith Friedman.
1ST ed. —Warwick, NY : Moo Press, 2005.

p. ; cm. (One incredible dog!)
Audience: ages 4-8.

Summary: Readers join search and rescue dog Boone to learn about the good things search and rescue dogs do for people every day.

ISBN 0-9724853-9-2
[ISBN-13: 978-0-9724853-9-5]

1. Dogs—Rescue Dogs—Juvenile literature.
2. Working Dogs—Juvenile literature.
3. Dogs—Training—Juvenile literature.
4. Search and rescue operations—Juvenile literature. 5. [Rescue work.]
I. Friedman, Judith. II. Title.

SF428.55 .W55 2005   2005920373
363.34/81/083—dc22   CIP

For information on permissions to reproduce, or about this and other Moo Press titles, please e-mail info@MooPress.com or write to Moo Press, Inc.

PO Box 54

Warwick, NY 10990.

To order copies of this book, please visit our Web site at www.MooPress.com or your local bookstore. For more information on search and rescue dogs, contact either the National Association for Search and Rescue at www.nasar.org, American Rescue Dog Association at www.ardainc.org, or Boone's website at www.SSARbloodhounds.org.

Manufactured in the United States of America.

Published by Moo Press an imprint of Keene Publishing Warwick, New York.

Dedicated with deep gratitude to my wife, Sue, for the hard work and long hours she spent helping to bring Boone's story to these pages.

— C.W.

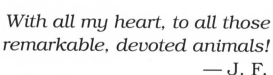

With all my heart, to all those remarkable, devoted animals!
— J. F.

In honor of our children, Sara and Drew, and their ever lasting love and respect for animals.
— Marylynn and Andy Gladstein[1]

[1]Summit Search and Rescue (SSAR) thanks Marylynn and Andy Gladstein for their generous donation, making this book possible, which will provide funding for the many needs of our search and rescue dogs and the SSAR operating expenses.

"Remember last summer when a tornado touched down outside of town?" Terri asks. Hands go up all over Mrs. Carpenter's fourth grade classroom.

"The sky turned really black and the wind roared," a tall girl says.

"It ripped a big tree out of our front lawn!" a freckle-faced boy exclaims.

"Many buildings were damaged," Terri says. "The roof of one house caved in and a lady was trapped under the rubble!"

"I bet she was scared!" another girl says.

"She was," Terri replies, "but Boone found her quickly!"

All eyes turn to a big but friendly-looking dog lying on the floor. His name is Daniel Boone. Most folks call him Boone.

He is a Search and Rescue dog.

He helps find people who are lost or hiding.

Search and Rescue dogs must have a very good sense of smell and be in good shape. They do a lot of running and walking. Sometimes they work for many hours.

For Boone, being a Search and Rescue dog is fun. It's like playing hide-and-seek, except Boone never gets to hide. He is always the "seeker."

Boone learned this game from Terri and Jim when he was only ten weeks old. They would take turns running away from Boone, then reward him with tasty treats and praise when he would follow.

As Boone grew bigger, he learned how to play this game while wearing a special work harness. Terri and Jim made the game harder by hiding from Boone. Boone had to use his nose to find them.

Boone learned to play this game in many different places:
    factories,
    train stations,
    construction sites,
    city streets,
    country paths,
    and even at lakes and rivers!

Boone was trained to do his work in any kind of weather. People don't just get lost on sunny and warm days!

Terri and Jim love to visit schools to tell children about Search and Rescue dogs and share important safety tips.

"Don't wander away from your parents or the adults you are with," Terri says.

"If you do have permission to go somewhere by yourself, go directly there and stay there until you get picked up," Jim adds.

"And it's a good idea to carry a whistle with you at all times," Terri explains, "just in case something unexpected happens and you get separated from your parents."

"Why?" Mrs. Carpenter asks.

"Because if you need to call for help, your voice might get tired and whistles can be heard farther," Terri answers.

Next, everyone goes outside to play Boone's special game of hide-and-seek. Several students hide while Terri distracts Boone.

It doesn't matter where they go:

behind trees,

under bushes,

or on top of the sliding board.

Boone finds them each and every time!

The children love Boone and give him lots of hugs before he leaves. Boone loves them too, and wags his tail.

After visiting the school, it's time for Boone's daily swim. On the way to Lake Chimi, Jim's cell phone rings. BRRRRING! It's the police department.

An eight-year-old girl named Maria Diaz is missing and the police want to know if Boone can help find her.

"We'll be right there," Jim replies.

A few minutes later, their van squeals to a stop in front of Maria's house. Two police cars are parked in the driveway.

"Thanks for coming," Officer Grant tells Terri and Jim.

"Nothing is more important than finding a lost girl," Jim replies as he snaps on Boone's special work harness.

Maria's mom opens her mouth to say something, but she begins to cry.

Terri puts her arm around her shoulder and says,"It's going to be all right."

"What does Maria look like?" Jim asks Officer Grant.

"She has black hair and brown eyes," the policeman answers. "And she was wearing blue shorts and a white shirt."

"To get her scent, Boone will need to sniff something that belongs to Maria," Jim says.

"Will her bicycle do?" Mrs. Diaz asks.

"That'll be fine," Jim replies.

Boone sniffs Maria's bike.

"Boone," Jim commands, "Find."

All Search and Rescue dogs have a search word. *Find* is Boone's word. When he hears it, he knows it's time to play his special game of hide-and-seek.

Boone begins to move.

"Looks like your dog is heading for the woods," Officer Grant says.

Jim nods and keeps a firm grip on the leash.

Boone leads the search team through rows and rows of leafy trees. Old leaves and twigs crunch under their feet. A couple of minutes later, Boone stops and sniffs an old tire.

"Boone's telling us that Maria's been here," Jim explains as thunder rumbles in the distance.

Deeper and deeper into the woods they go.

A few raindrops begin to plop around them.

Boone keeps walking and sniffing, but there is still no sign of Maria. Rain falls more heavily as they follow Boone.

Suddenly, Boone stops in front of an old concrete pipe.

"WOOF-WOOF! WOOF-WOOF! WOOF!"

Terri kneels down and looks inside.

Sitting in the pipe is a girl with black hair and brown eyes.

"Hi. Are you Maria Diaz?" Terri asks.

"Yes," a tearful Maria answers.

Maria scrambles out of the pipe on her hands and knees. Soon Mrs. Diaz is reunited with Maria.

"Thank you so much for finding my daughter!" she tells Terri and Jim.

"Don't thank us," Jim replies. "Boone did all the work!"

Mrs. Diaz kneels down and hugs Boone's neck.

"Boone, you are one incredible dog!" she says.

"Make room for me!" Maria says, and hugs Boone too.

J im glances up at the sky. "The sun is coming out again. I guess we'll be able to take Boone for his…"

BRRRRING! Jim's cell phone rings before he can say, "swim."

He listens closely and nods his head. "Sure," he says. "We'll be right out."

After ending the call, Jim tells Terri, "A man didn't show up at his grandson's birthday party, but his car did."

"That sounds strange," Terri says as they get into their van.

The missing person's family greets Jim and Terri with worried faces.

"My dad was supposed to be here two hours ago," Mr. Stewart says.

"It's so unlike him," Mrs. Stewart adds. "He's always on time."

"Are you going to find Grandpa Archie?" Billy Stewart asks.

"We'll do our best," Jim says. "If you and your parents can show me your grandpa's car, that will be a big help."

They walk around the corner and Billy points to a big white car. "There it is," he says.

Boone sniffs the driver's side door and then Jim says, "Find."

Boone heads down the busy city sidewalk.

One—two—three blocks.

He stops in front of a movie theater and begins to pull Jim toward the door.

Inside, sleeping in the back row, is Grandpa Archie.

"I came into town early to buy a gift," he explains after being gently awakened. "Then I had some extra time so I decided to see a movie."

The old gentleman laughs. "The movie was so boring I fell asleep!"

When Billy sees Grandpa Archie walking toward the restaurant, he runs to meet him.

"Sorry I missed your birthday party," his grandpa says.

"I don't care about that!" Billy says. "You're here now!"

Billy puts a party hat on Boone's head. "Thanks for finding my grandpa," he says.

Everyone laughs.

Suddenly, a policewoman runs around the corner.

"Did you see a man run by?" she asks, a little out of breath.

"I didn't see anyone," Billy says.

Mr. and Mrs. Stewart shake their heads.

"Well, he grabbed a lady's purse and took off in this direction," the policewoman explains.

"Why don't we put Boone on the case?" Billy asks.

"That's an excellent idea," Terri responds.

"Do you have something for Boone to sniff?" Jim asks.

"He dropped his hat back there," the policewoman answers as she leads them back to the hat.

With one sniff of the hat, and the sound of the word *find*, Boone springs into action.

Boone dashes across the street into the park.

Hiding under an old bandstand is the purse snatcher!

When he sees the policewoman, he tries to run away, but she soon catches him.

"Thank you very much," the policewoman says to Terri and Jim.

"You're welcome," Terri responds.

"Anytime we're needed," Jim says.

"And thank you!" she adds, patting Boone's head.

Moments later, after a busy day, Boone is finally on his way for a swim in the cool waters of Lake Chimi.

Search and Rescue dogs are helpful friends who do their special work after earthquakes, tornadoes, hurricanes, avalanches, building collapses, terrorist attacks, and other disasters.

They also play a vital role in finding missing children and adults; and apprehending criminals on the run. Some Search and Rescue dogs even help scuba divers do water rescues!

If you'd like to learn more about Search and Rescue dogs, here are some nonprofit organizations that can provide you with more information:

- ◆ National Association for Search and Rescue (www.nasar.org)
- ◆ American Rescue Dog Association (www.ardainc.org)
- ◆ Boone's Summit Search and Rescue (www.SSARbloodhounds.org)